Never Kiss an
Alligator!

Never Kiss an Alligator!

Colleen Stanley Bare

Photographs by the author

A PUFFIN UNICORN

To
Karen and Warren

Acknowledgments

Melvin Gentry and personnel at the Gatorland Zoo in Orlando, Florida; and the staffs at the Alligator Farm in St. Augustine, Florida, and at Florida's Everglades National Park.

PUFFIN BOOKS
Published by the Penguin Group
Penguin Books USA Inc., 375 Hudson Street, New York, New York 10014, U.S.A.
Penguin Books Ltd, 27 Wrights Lane, London W8 5TZ, England
Penguin Books Australia Ltd, Ringwood, Victoria, Australia
Penguin Books Canada Ltd, 10 Alcorn Avenue, Toronto, Ontario, Canada M4V 3B2
Penguin Books (N.Z.) Ltd, 182–190 Wairau Road, Auckland 10, New Zealand
Penguin Books Ltd, Registered Offices: Harmondsworth, Middlesex, England

First published in the United States by Cobblehill Books,
an affiliate of Dutton Children's Books,
a division of Penguin Books USA Inc., 1989
Published by Puffin Books, 1994

Library of Congress Catalog Card Number: 92-62835
ISBN 0-14-055257-X
Designer: Charlotte Staub
Printed in the United States of America
10   9   8

Never Kiss an Alligator! is also available
in hardcover from Cobblehill Books

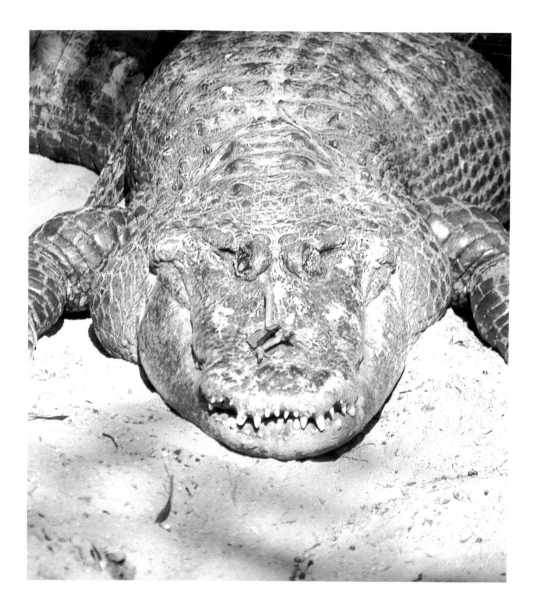

Never kiss an alligator,
    hug an alligator,
        pat, poke, push, hit, kick,
or even touch an alligator,
because alligators bite!

When you meet an alligator,
usually at a zoo,
what should you do?

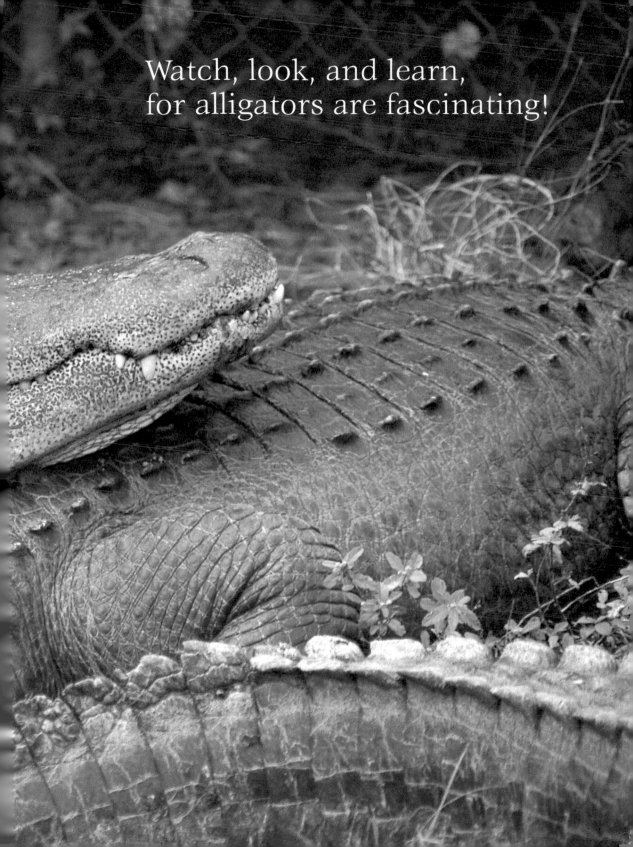

Watch, look, and learn,
for alligators are fascinating!

Alligators are ancient,
and lived when the dinosaurs lived
about two hundred million years
ago.

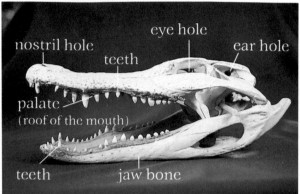

The name alligator is from a
Spanish word "el lagarto,"
which means "the lizard."
Lizards do look like miniature
alligators.

Alligator lizard

Florida alligators

Alligators are found in only two
parts of the world:
a few in eastern China,
most in the warm
southeastern United States,
especially Louisiana and Florida.

Alligators live in water,
beside water
half in and half
out of water.

They stay in ponds,
beside an algae-covered pond
in an algae-covered pond

in swamps, marshes, lakes,
   rivers, streams,
and sometimes in people's
   swimming pools, fish ponds,
   and in water on golf courses.

Alligators can stay under the
water at least an hour, holding
their breaths.
In dry seasons
they may dig deep holes in
the ground until they find
water.
These "gator holes" are also used
by other wildlife.

Alligators aren't crocodiles, and
crocodiles aren't alligators, although
they belong to the same family,
called Crocodilia (Crock-o-DILLy-uh).

Alligator

Crocodile

Alligators have broad, rounded noses.

Crocodiles have longer, skinnier noses.

Alligators' lower teeth don't show when their mouths are closed.

Crocodiles' lower teeth do show when their mouths are closed.

Alligator

Crocodile

Crocodiles are crankier, bolder,
     fiercer,
and move faster than alligators,
so certainly, definitely, without a
     doubt,
you should never kiss a
     crocodile's snout!

Alligators have huge mouths,
with about eighty sharp teeth
for snapping and snatching:
insects, fish, small animals,
birds, turtles, frogs, snakes,
sometimes stones, bottle caps,
cans,

and even people, if people
tease or get in the way.

Alligator teeth fall out and get
replaced by new ones,
up to three thousand in a
fifty-year lifetime.

Alligators have short, stubby legs
for walking on land
and, for a brief distance, can run
as fast as you can.

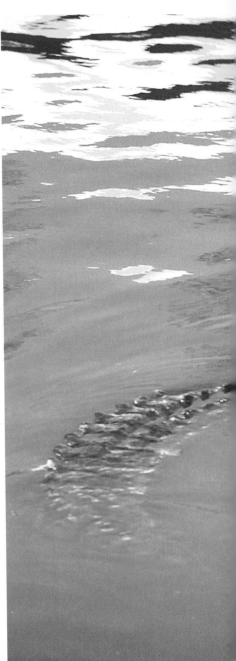

Alligators have long,
scaly tails for
swimming in water.

The faster they swish their tails,
the faster they can swim.

Alligators' eyes, ears, and noses
are on top of their heads,
so they can see, hear, and smell
while they hide in the water
to watch for meals.

The Florida Everglades

Where is the alligator?

There is the alligator.

Alligators are reptiles,
so their body temperatures are
the same as the air or the
water around them.
They lie around looking lazy
to get warm in the sun,
to get cool in the shade.

Three-inch alligator egg

Like most reptiles, mother
    alligators lay eggs.
Babies hatch out of the thirty to
    sixty eggs
    in about ten weeks.

Newborn alligators are eight to
nine inches long
and have sharp little teeth that
nip and bite.

Baby alligator

So never kiss a baby alligator,
either!

One-year-old alligator

Baby alligators grow about one
foot a year until age six.
They continue to grow slowly
most of their lives,
to around thirteen feet for
males,
nine feet for females.

Baby alligators have many
enemies: raccoons, skunks,
bobcats, snakes, river otters,
and big birds.

Raccoon

Alligators make noises:
babies hiss and grunt,
adults hiss, bellow, and roar.

Some alligators are kept in zoos where, during "gator shows," they leap out of water to grab raw chicken and fish,

"perform"
with the
zookeepers,

and, always muzzled, get held by
children.

Two-year-old alligator

Alligators have thick, leathery, shiny, scaly skins
that some humans want to make into purses, shoes, belts, and wallets.
Man is the alligator's greatest enemy.

Alligator hide

Never kiss an alligator,
because alligators aren't for
kissing or hugging
or for shooting or killing.

They are to watch, study, admire,
and to preserve, protect, and
respect
as survivors of the dinosaur age.